MAKE WAY FOR YOU

TIPS FOR GETTING OUT OF YOUR OWN WAY

VOL. 1

TONY ORTIZ

MAKE WAY FOR YOU (Tips for Getting Out of Your Own Way)

Spun Today Publishing

www.TonyOrtizAuthor.com

eBook ISBN: 979-8-9886622-5-9

Paperback ISBN: 979-8-9886622-6-6

Hardcover ISBN: 979-8-9886622-7-3

Audiobook ISBN: 979-8-9886622-8-0

1. Main category—Self Help / Creativity

2. Other category—Self Help / Journal Writing

3. Other category—Self Help / Motivational

First Edition

BOOKS BY THE AUTHOR

Fractal – A Time Travel Tale (A Novel)
Melted Cold (A Collection of Short Stories)

Check out the following for even more reading:
Free-Writing: www.SpunToday.com/freewriting
Short Stories: www.SpunToday.com/shortstories

This is the first volume in a collection of freely written thoughts that helped me get through some of my own personal barriers and bullshit. My hope is that they can help you in a similar way.

Here's to all of those dormant creators out there.

For My Mother

Epigraph

"Our planet is a lonely speck in the great enveloping cosmic dark. In our obscurity, in all this vastness, there is no hint that help will come from elsewhere to save us from ourselves. The Earth is the only world known so far to harbor life. There is nowhere else, at least in the near future, to which our species could migrate. Visit, yes. Settle, not yet. Like it or not, for the moment the Earth is where we make our stand."

— Carl Sagan, *Pale Blue Dot* - from a Public Lecture delivered on October 13th, 1994 at Cornell University

LET YOURSELF OUT

he greatest version of yourself is dying to come out. It's practically oozing out of your pores. But you stifle it. You stop it. You postpone it. You get in your own way, piling up hurdle upon hurdle, instead of clearing the path to allow you to rise from the ashes of your unfulfilled self. Break that trend and stop that trajectory. You're digging a hole so deep for yourself that before you know it - will become the grave of the life that could've been. Build up to the you that you need to become. We elevate each other by lifting ourselves. It's your duty, your calling *not* to squander it. We're all in this together but it begins and ends with you. Don't waste that talent. Nurture it and allow it to have the everlasting ripple-effect impact that it was meant to have. Throw a pebble of effort into the pool of the universe each day ... and lets get started.

HOW WILL YOU USE
YOUR 24 HOURS?

❧

*C*atch up mode. You can't really make up for lost time ... it's over, it's done. But you can absolutely change your downward trajectory and begin to aim upward. Get yourself into a groove. Into the zone. Your zone. Where only you can be. A one person, unique membership. A one-of-a-kind place whose replica doesn't exist. It can't exist. You make it what it is, what it can be and what it can't be. No more excuses. Find the time. **Make** the time for whatever it is that you need to do for you. Whatever goal you have. Begin to put in the work ... now. No, literally right now. We all get 24 hours each day ... how will you **choose** to use yours?

DON'T FEAR SUCCESS

⚜

*Y*ou can't be afraid of success. That's what it is, isn't it. Isn't it? I mean it's the essence of fears, self-made obstacles and barriers. You shouldn't be afraid of success, but you can't be predominantly driven by it either. You need to be indifferent to it. It's an added bonus at best. I guess that's where the; 'it's the journey – not the destination', saying comes from. The guiding light-of the North Star. The vitamin B6 that converts L-Tryptophan and 5-HTP into serotonin producing catalysts. You need to keep it at bay in terms of wanting it, or thinking that you need it, while simultaneously wanting and needing it. Achieve your type of success through apathetic hard work.

MEMORIES

*M*emories are awesome. They are at the source of everything. They're happening around us as we speak ... waiting to come to fruition down the line, to become what they were destined to be. Memories are the past they are history. History is a memory. The history we read about in textbooks, the history we have in our relationships with one another ... all memories. Conjured up in our minds in endlessly looping streams. Infinitely and unpredictably present in the database of our minds. Memories are brought to the forefront of our minds ... to the present, via reminiscing, via reading, via photography, via home videos. Memories tie together our past with our present and help in shaping our futures. The tools, by which memories are invoked, are plentiful and invaluable. They come in all shapes, sizes, colors and textures. Good/bad, dark/light, fun/boring, stressful/blissful. Make a conscious effort today, to make tomorrows memories blissful, but know that the humbling memories are just as important.

NOBODY IS NECESSARILY NECESSARY

Nobody is worth making you feel like you can't be you. Ever. It's one thing to reserve judgment out of courtesy, or to act a certain way towards a relative, older person, authority figure, etc. – out of respect. It's another thing to feel shamed into not expressing certain ideas, thoughts, concerns and input. Anyone that is stifling you in that way, doesn't need to be around you. You make that decision. It's not case-by-case, it's not circumstantial. Nobody is necessarily necessary. Don't get me wrong, constructive criticism is essential … and someone coming at you from a good place and pointing out something you did or are doing wrong, is of benefit to our development and growth as individuals. But the negative, ego-driven, hate/animosity undertone is not only unnecessary, it's detrimental. It has an attritional effect on you as a person. But the good news is that letting people in and cutting people out, is completely under your discretion.

TAKING THE POSITIVE
OR NEGATIVE ROUTE

hings can always be worse, but they can always be better too. It's up to you to decide which route to take when you reach that fork in your decision – making road. Of course things are going to happen that are out of your control or that set you off course and take you in a different direction than you intended to be going in ... but that's when your resolve and dedication to your path kick into over-drive ... or doesn't. It may seem nonsensical, but your mood and general outlook play a general guiding role in that. If you decide to beat yourself up and dwell on the negativity, you're refusing to move forward. Even if you think you are, or are capable of still moving forward, you're not. You're fooling yourself. That negativity snowballs and grabs other negative aspects of your life and areas that you feel you can be doing better in, and brings them to the fore-front of your mind. Misery loves company, right? Negativity comes in all different shapes and sizes, colors and textures, so it may be hard to recognize ... but you can train yourself to. Cleanse yourself of it wherever and whenever possible. Hate, jealousy, envy, greed, self-doubt, self-loathing, are all forms of negativity. – They all exist but don't have to. Flip it on them. Substitute in; love, trust, admiration, generosity, belief in yourself, pride - But not the selfish stubborn kind, the motivating 'I can do this' kind. The former is just negativity disguised. Just like the negativity snowballs, so does the positivity. Set the course of which way it goes, by the choices you make. And again, there's no exact right and wrong, good and bad. There's just right & wrong and good & bad – *for you*. You decide what that means. Do away with the negative thoughts and actions, negative beliefs and people. Each and every one of those are dispensable if you're trying to be positive … they're just negativity disguised. Does positivity disguise itself too?

KNOW YOUR SIDE AND THEIRS

*S*urround yourself with like-minded individuals ... but know the other side well enough to find comfort in yours. There's a huge difference between confirmation bias and being like-minded. Similarities exist of course, but they couldn't be further apart from each other. They have the common denominator of surrounding yourself with a person or idea that resonates with you, but for different reasons. With confirmation bias, you're sort of searching for validation. Attaching yourself to someone or something that you feel (maybe even genuinely) you should because it supports you or your thoughts in some way. But with having an underlying fear of being wrong, or 'on the wrong side' of something or someone, being misinformed, etc. There are holes in confirmation bias. It's not sturdy. There's a fake-ness or incompleteness to it. The foundation is fucked up. It won't hold. It can't. Being like-minded works. – Or can work rather. It's set up differently. With Positivity. It's a unanimous decision. It's being compatible. Having similar tastes, desires, fears, etc. Empathy versus sympathy.

It's fitting. If you still don't see the difference, then look harder. Inside you. It's there.

AVOID A PURPOSELESS JOURNEY

I spent a large part of my life motivated by the wrong type of motivation. The wrong type of 'what success meant'. Always falling short of unattainable goals (while in that mind set) because the litmus test to gauge that success was and is a bad indicator. We shouldn't allow money and materials to dictate our drive ... that's a purposeless journey. Those things are and should always be treated as being an added plus, a byproduct. Aside from the essentials (which to me are a given); Family, health, true Friendships ... I've found myself realizing what true success is. What it is and means to me. To others it may be different, or not yet realized. Having a positive outlook is key. That's a prerequisite. Self-awareness and being centered. Knowing yourself, what you want and don't want and actually acting accordingly ... not just going with the flow and waiting for change to come to you. Being aware of those around you and how you and your actions or inactions affect them. Dedication to craft ... whatever it is that makes you feel like you, not the 'you' that you or others think you're *supposed* to be. That can be anything; writing, reading, drawing, painting, watching movies, filming movies, creating music, arts & crafts, jogging ... literally anything ... studying, exercising, spirituality, volunteering, learning a particular language or learning more about a particular thing you heard about that peaked your curiosity ... **anything**, but make sure you own it! Make it yours. Make it your thing – but only if and when you're able (which we all are) and willing to do it for you. That's how I find my happiness, my success. How you choose to measure it from there is just as important too. Because those tangible results are measurable and quantifiable but this in itself isn't. You can consider it to be limited in that respect, or find it to be limit*less*. Most importantly though, I realized that it is an endless work-in-progress which is my general outlook on life. It can't ever be seen as a scapegoat or some sort of rationalization for not achieving some arbitrary financial goal. That's that wrong motivation talking. The process, the outlook, is the goal in and of itself. Sure we have needs and wants and desires, but think in terms of: 'If you build it – they will come' ... without that truly trivial end goal as your motivation.

SILVER LININGS

*E*ight days is eight days too many…if I'm going to make this a serious endeavor I can't take so long in between sessions to work on my craft. Neither should you. We can't just work when we feel a spark of inspiration to do so. With that approach we won't ever accomplish shit. The silver lining is that eight is my favorite number, I guess. You have to try and find the positive in any and every situation that life confronts you with. Not an excuse, but a positive. Any positive … yup, even in those types of situations; bad health, shitty hands dealt, death. – These are the times where silver linings are even more scarce and that much more necessary. They say we learn and grow from our mistakes, mishaps and losses, but that's not an automatic sequence of events. It's a choice to do so, or not to do so, and that choice is 100% at your discretion, regardless of the influences of outside events and/or obstacles. Go left, right or even straight … but make your bed and lie in it.

WHAT DOES YOUR
MUSIC SOUND LIKE?

writers-block-session, is what I'm going to call these. When I have nothing to say but that nothing still needs to come out. I already have more than I thought I would. The pen just needs to touch the paper. If even only for practice-sake. For writing endurance. For better penmanship at the very least. The point is that work alone, yields something. "A life lived for Art, is never a life wasted". [1] The pen touching the paper is like the needle of a vinyl record player. The paper is the record and the 'muse' feeding the words is the music. Without fail, it's always there for you when you make yourself able to do the work and put your pen to the paper. What's your music sound like? I'm fine tuning mine.

---

1. This Lyric is from the "Ten Thousand Hours" song by Macklemore

GET UP FOR YOUR WIN

*oming back from behind. That moment when you're down & out and then rise back up from that place. That all engulfing but motivating place. You feel trapped. The walls are closing in. But that moment triggers something inside of you that makes you address the situation at hand and make the decisions and choices necessary to push those walls back out. To get up when you're down, and come back for the win … your win.

NOBODY ELSE CAN BECOME YOU

*Y*ou are what you feel you're supposed to be. You just need to become it. You're a collection of all your experiences, knowledge, dreams, hopes and desires, but only you can combine them all in becoming the 'you', that you know you are. Nobody and nothing can become it for you, and more importantly, nobody can *ever* become the you that you're supposed to be. Ever. They may achieve similar goals, but in *their* way. Not yours. Not becoming you, is depriving both yourself and the world. Don't be that type of selfish. Embrace the type of selflessness that the 'you' that you want to become wants you to embrace. Start there. Start with giving. Start with giving of you.

FIND YOURSELF

⚜

otivated for betterment. Improving yourself and those around you. Practice makes perfect, but only when coupled with passion, dedication and discipline can you really bring the concept full circle and to fruition. Staying on track, even if you veer off a bit ... but on the general track of your choosing. You're finally on the right train. The right mind state. The right chi. Capture it, without the option of letting it slip. Today, like no other day, you find you.

DON'T MISS OUT
ON A BETTER YOU

❦

*W*hat changes you? Are all parts and aspects of you susceptible to change – or is there a core, unalterable "you"? That sounds more like it to me. The best of both worlds. You have what makes you, uniquely 'you', and you also have the absorbent ability to accept additional knowledge and change accordingly. What causes these changes? – Not as in; 'what events cause this'? - but as in; 'what within you evokes this green-light effect in which you *allow* certain events or experiences to effect you in some way, shape or form. What within you allows a book to have such a profound connection, that it opens up your eyes to never before considered angles and interpretations. What allows the conversation of a Podcast to expand your mind? What allows (un-skewed) data from a recent news article, to aid in shaping a Political opinion? It's all a question of what do you let in to truly analyze and objectively tackle. It all boils down to a choice … make yourself open enough not to miss out on a better you.

GET OUT OF YOUR OWN WAY

ometimes you go for it, and sometimes you don't. When you don't, that pesky 'what if' feeling and thought, like a thorn at the side of your mind, births regret. On the flip side, when you actually do go for it, whether the outcome turns out as hoped or the complete opposite occurs, you have a lasting sense of accomplishment. A certain type of pride. A pride fused with relief for facing and staring down something that scared you. So why the fuck not go for it each and every consciously feasible time? What's stopping you except for yourself? Get out of your own way.

WHAT DO YOU WANT?

❧

What are your true wants and desires? Your dreams and aspirations? Not what you think you should be or become. Or what family, friends and others think you ought to be. But what you truly want for yourself. Where does that come from? What is that? Genetic predisposition? The concept of "The Muse"? Who knows? When you are able to listen to that 'voice' though, things seem much more fluid. A moment of clarity shines through and illuminates your path in life, casting a shadow on self-doubt and disbelief. Allowing you to see the possibilities that lay before you. That moment allows you to distinguish between the positive and negative options. A seamless transient moment. The next step is on you. The difficult part. You already have the map, but now you need to follow the coordinates to your destination. Put in the type of work that is worthy of taking part in he journey towards it. Time is a constraining illusion. Don't let it deter you from going towards your wants and desires.

PARA ATRAS NI PARA
COGER IMPULSO

⁂

*S*tay on course no matter what. There will be bumps and bruises, twists and turns along the way ... there's no way to change that ... go through them. Get through them. Your mind is set. Your goals have been determined. No matter the obstacle(s), the length of time and/or space between you and your plans ... your general trajectory should never change. Shuck and jive when you need to, pero "para atras ni para coger impulso". [1] You'll eventually get to where you want/need to be. Whether it be by realizing that the journey *is* the destination, or by experiencing the destination prolifically reflecting the fruitfulness of the journey. But don't just stay the course and wait for "it" to come to you. Put in the work. Tons of it. A sickening amount if need be ... but make yourself earn it. Nothing worthwhile comes easy, nor should it.

---

1. This is a Hispanic expression that in the Dominican Republic stands for; "always move forward, never backwards – not even to gain momentum."

BE PRESENT IN YOUR JOURNEY

*F*rom the deepest depths of the lows, to the upmost heights of the highs. The intricate labyrinth of endless twists and turns in between with infinite paths to each, or towards each of these polar destinations. But while your eyes are on the prize, don't miss the forest for looking at the trees. Embrace the journey. Stop and look around once in a while. There's not only one option for you. One path. Even if there is one specific goal that you have for yourself … you can get there a myriad of ways. After you get where you're going, you'll look back on your quest and realize that the picture it paints with the memories of your life, is a priceless work of art that is yours and only yours. No brush and canvass combo has ever or will ever create it quite like you did. Appreciate and savor all that is and all that will be you.

WANTING VS. DOING

hat is the difference between wanting to do, and actually doing? What is the catalyst that sparks change? Where exactly is that switch, and how can we switch it? I guess it varies from person to person and is definitely situational, but what's the 'rule of thumb'? Is there even one? I strongly believe that what is wanted and envisioned, can be worked on and cultivated. Almost all scenarios share, one main ingredient; 'hard work'. But it can and will be frustrating to actually get on the path towards it. Just know and keep in mind that doing things like this are definitely steps in that direction. Reading about it, writing. Every time you draw a draft in your sketch book or practice a lyric, you're doing it ... just don't stop.

BE DESERVING OF A
PERFECT MOMENT

*I*t's pretty instant. As soon as the pen touches the paper. It seems to burst out. It all begins to flow. Thoughts of nothing become something. Or maybe they stay nothing. None-the-less, they come out almost as if to serve a purpose. Not really going 'where they've always belonged' or 'returning home' per say, but sort of like they're an important catalyst or precursor to something more. Something not yet in existence but needing to be. – Not in a grandiose type of way, but in a 'for me' type of way. "Whatever will be, will be", and whatever it is will take practice. Practice makes perfect and 'perfection' requires work so that when opportunity, preparation and luck triangulate and cross paths … the moment can be guided and executed the way it deserves to be. Be deserving of a perfect moment.

STICK TO IT

What I want to write about seems to be there. Waiting eagerly to be written about. Through the bushes, in the distance. It's there, I know it. I don't see it, in the literal sense but I feel it, in the un-quantifiable sense. It's there, like the anticipation and excitement of a kid on Christmas morning. Percolating. I feel like I'm slowly but surely getting thru the shrubbery. The obstacles seem to be fading albeit at a very sluggish pace. Step by step. Slow and steady wins the race.

MAKE WAY FOR YOU

ight for your right to write. The way you would gasp for air if you couldn't breathe. The way you would quench your thirst if your throat were parched. It's an untapped, god given ability. Your right to freely express yourself, to yourself and to others. To get out of your own way enough, to make way for you. The depths of the inner you are infinite, and this is how you tap into it. Write. Move whatever is in your way, out of the way and write. Do this to the point where only writing is in the way of writing. Create. Put the pen to the paper, the text on the screen, whichever you prefer. – But let it flow. Your cup is permanently 'runneth over' ... so let it flow. Tap into the deepness that is you, to unveil what in hindsight will only feel foreign. Unleash the unconscious thoughts that are spiraling toward consciousness, to synergistically create aspects of our lives, that are so infinitely you. Fight for your right to write, and write because you have the right to fight.

LET IT SHINE

I have greatness within me, and so do you. We all do, really. Will it come out, shone through and expose itself, is the question. Will it give way to itself, in place of vulnerability? Will it shine bright without fright? Will you let it? Will you allow it? Will it advise you, guide you? Shine through the way it's supposed to? I don't know about you, but for me it's going to. You should see to it that it does so for you too. It's your responsibility and you owe it to yourself and all others. Greatness isn't yours to keep for yourself. Its essence is exoteric in nature. Meant for blanket distribution. Find your medium, your style, your voice ... your choice. Own it. Hone it. Fine-tune it. Get out of your own way and use it.

CREATE ART

℘

*A*rt is infinitely eternal. Why? – Because it is 100% subjective. Writing of any kind, music of any kind, painting of any kind, acting of any kind … it's all ironically timeless. Ironically, because by origin, it is reflective of and encapsulated within a certain time, but it doesn't necessarily reflect that time period. Or it can to me, but it not to you and vice versa. Fractal influences on the creator speak to both its plurality and singularity. Poetry, theatre, fiction, hip-hop, non-fiction, thrillers, rock, free-writing, jazz, drawing, research writing, bachata, pottery … whatever the medium, there's an audience. A following. Like-minded individuals that find comfort and belonging and inspiration and motivation within the shared Art. And not because they necessarily find the same things in common with each other, but because something resonates with them. It may not be the same thing(s) that resonate with you, or maybe it is…but it's a subjective connection non-the-less. The way we marvel at the wonders of the world with awed admiration or ancient texts, is the way that todays Art will transcend time, along with all previous forms of Art. It's an important, humbling connection we share with each other, with our past, present and future. Whatever Art is to you … continue to create.

INACTION SPEAKS VOLUMES

What is it that interrupts our grand plans? That stops our dreams from coming to fruition? What is it that blocks us from rising up to the challenge of our self-rival? Sure life gets in the way of living, but we allow it to. Why is that? What's really going on? Are we scared to achieve? Scared to try and fail? Ignorant of the, 'if at first you don't succeed...' concept? We need to start getting out of our own way. We're tripping ourselves up. Busy "living" our lives, but not living life. How interesting is it, that the masses, including myself, seem to be satisfied with this existence? Not internally, but from the outside looking in, the inaction speaks volumes. So from that perspective, when measuring action; wanting to do something but doing nothing about it, is equivalent to never wanting to do something at all. Both trains of thought have the same outcome ... nothing. Why do we allow some thoughts and goals to break thru and manifest themselves in a tangible way? Can we control the proverbial bouncer at the doorway of our thoughts? By assuming the position of that bouncer ... I think so, but currently that's only an internal thought.

I'VE GOT THAT
STAGNANT FEELING

*aking on tasks upon tasks to essentially push back the eventual (if ever) completion date of prior tasks, is a key cause of the problem. That feeling of stagnation. That's where it stems from. You're hoarding distractions in the form of a to-do list. So how do you fix the issue? Set a due date for all tasks, and plan to get them all done by said date ... and those that aren't get deleted or un-tasked. This could be effective. On different levels, not just sufficing the lists, but in letting go of the dependency of them. Because if they're not being effective and consistently completed, they're having a negative, weighing-down effect on you. What's the point of them then? Now, what happens post 'list-apocalypse'? What protocol is put into place to prevent continual or future task hoarding? A running one week limit on all new tasks. D or D = done or deleted. Firmly followed. It may be worth an implementation. There are a slew of productivity apps, pen & paper to-do list tactics, etc. Pick *one* and get things done.

WHEN YOU GET THERE, DON'T
FORGET WHERE YOU CAME FROM

I believe in me, as you should believe in you. Call it pride, call it hubris, but I'm going to do this. I want what's coming to me, as long as I earn it. Why else would it be headed in my direction? Focus, hard work, discipline and dedicated passion will all combine to warrant self satisfaction. Rise to the occasion and seize the moment. Own it. Own everything that you do. It's done and is an unwavering part of you. It's all a series of building blocks and sometimes you have to go through the wrong to find the right fit. The pieces of the puzzle eventually come together and fall into place. – But don't forget and disgrace the spark that brought it into fruition. Every roaring flame has an initial spark. A place of origin. The base you need to embrace. The building block you need to hold up as your standard 'when you get there, don't forget where you came from'. Even when all is right and there's no end in sight … there's always a start of which you'll always be a part.

KEYS TO SUCCESS

ou have the *option* to *alt* your reality. It is within your *control*. You make a series of choices, some dependent and or influenced by other previous choices … but choices nonetheless. You may or may not be satisfied with your current station in life, but the ability to *shift* gears and change the general trajectory of your path, is on you. At the end of the day, you cannot *escape* your reality. But you can continuously create it. You can be calm and conservative, or wild and free. You can *start* off as one, and *return* to being the other. You can't ever *delete* what you've done but you can *enter* into agreements with yourself on not committing the same mistake twice, thrice or what have you. Good or bad and all the in between, it all adds up for each of us. – And in the end, we're all paying our own *tab*.

HOW WILL YOU HAVE
SPENT YOUR TIME?

s the world turns without an anticipated end, it births new life full of endless hope and potential, the likes of which are only paralleled by the relentless indiscriminate death that it inevitably leaves behind. A cycle that by definition goes full circle. A cycle fulfilling its purpose and simply doing what it's meant to do. Adopt that characteristic. That all beings and things, aside from us, seem to adopt and carry out as if there were no other way. Some of us are able to hone in that sense of purpose and live out our days in a way that gives our lives meaning and a sense of worth. Others of us allow the randomness of life to influence and interfere with our destiny. We give importance where it's unwarranted, instead of where it's lacking. When it's all said and done, the time will have passed, the world will have given its final turn with you on it, and the realization of your time will come full circle. How will you have spent your time?

CHANNEL AND AIM YOUR INTENT

*hy do we dodge things? Avoid situations? Prolong tasks? Elongate the path to a goal? To avoid the possible discomfort of facing it head-on and in a focused manor? When you detach yourself from whatever it is that you're putting off, for whatever reason ... you should be able to plainly see that dealing and taking care of whatever it is that is on that literal and or proverbial to-do list, is far less disconcerting than the constant reminder of the undone, un-attempted, un-satisfied task that on some level, remains lingering around. All the half starts, half-assed attempts, will do's, etc. Can easily be lumped into the category of un-done. Not completed, not accomplished. The exact opposite of what you want and where you want these things to be. That psychological application is and needs to be, the pre-cursor to the rational, practical application. Mind over matter. The thought before the act. Channel and aim your intent. Your focus. Your drive and persistence. Go after your goals with laser-like, surgical precision.

DON'T GET LOST IN THE HAZE

Dedication, passion. Love and a touch of necessity … what a powerful blend of emotions. Does a stronger mix exist? An alchemist couldn't yield more value than what that powerful combination is able to conjure. When tuned into the frequency at the 4-way cross-section of those emotions, your output is worthy of praise. It's beautiful. You put in the work and returned to you are the fruits of your labor in spades. Can you stay tuned in or do you stray? Is it a permanent situation or do you inevitably get lost in the haze?

DEVELOP A STRONG
FOUNDATION

~~~

*D*abbling in life. Where nothing feels quite right. Well, maybe not nothing, but some things. Enough aspects of your life left wanting and in need of focused attention. Some people, perhaps. Jobs, hobbies, interests. You skim the surface of all of the above, jumping from one thing to the next because you're busy with the details. Take a step back, enough of a step to gain the impulse needed to jump and dive into the thick of it. Whatever it is. Stop and look around. Give the wanting areas of your life some undivided attention. A caring affection. Living day to day pushing things off to the next day and then the one after that, is akin to financially, living paycheck to paycheck. It isn't healthy. Necessary? Maybe ... but probably not. The foundation is shaky, at best. Like plugging holes in a sinking ship. It can be, and should be more than that. Focus your time and attention to where you feel you want and need it to be. Dedicate and discipline yourself to that task. To develop that potentially life-changing trait. In the long run you can either be a jack of all trades – master of none, or embrace, nurture and flourish your potential(s), for "...if you know the way broadly, you will see it in everything"[1]

---

1. The Book of Five Rings - Miyamoto Musashi

ALLOW YOURSELF TO GROW

ou take from experiences what you're ready to allow yourself to use for growth and personal development. Personal being the operative word. That growth is self-defining yet has no exact definition. As long as your development and growth is not hindering anyone else's and you're expanding outwardly with the internalized version of your experiences as the fuel ... then you're doing what you need to be doing, for you. – Which down the line will translate into the capacity to 'do unto others'. Both positive and negative experiences can provide this outward growth. Don't think of growth in terms of expanding and contracting with positive and negatives influencing respectively. Instead think of both positive and negative experiences working towards the same goal. The absolute value of all experiences, positive or negative, increase your fluid growth like ripples in water, expanding ever outward. Allow yourself to grow.

DECIDE TO WALK YOUR PATH

*S*tarting over is an interesting concept. Refreshing at its core. Letting go and coming to terms with, and being ok with, what is over. What is done with. Humbling as it may be, it is in essence fueling of hubris. Turning a new leaf and wiping the slate clean, gives you a new blank slate to work with. A blank slate whose plans, predictions, and expectations of the future are infinite. You can do anything now right? What stopped you before though? The mental blocks and obstacles you put in your own way. Trials and tribulations you'll have to encounter on any path you walk … so why not encounter the ones on the path you want to be walking? Seems cliché, but the difference in either path is simply *deciding* to walk it. If something as a New Year, or Birthday or some other milestone you set for yourself and achieve becomes the jump off point or catalyst, so be it. That's completely secondary and not nearly as important as the actual follow through. Let it, and you shone through. New Beginnings.

MAKE IT FOR YOU

Take all the pain and suffering, discomfort and fear, and allow it to pour out of you in this form here. Mold it and sculpt it into something that's yours. Create an esoteric expression of self that is soothing to your soul. To the very fiber of your being. Embrace it. Raise it. Cherish it. Nurture it. It's you in the rawest form of you. After all the onion-like layers, past the influence and self-doubt. Before the judgment takes its stranglehold. In its purest form. Expand that positive pure output that will pour within itself to fulfill and quench the thirst of your hopes, your dreams and your desires. Go for it.

BE AHEAD OF THE EIGHT BALL

*S*ometimes you need a spark to set things in motion, to get you going. You can find that proverbial spark in different things. Different situations and events. Internalize that and realize that the spark is really coming from you. Giving importance, or personifying something to the point that it *becomes* that spark, is a self-realization of an unmet necessity in you. A want, a desire. You allow yourself to feel and understand that void while implementing a plan sparked by that very same need, in order to fill it. If you can summon up that spark at will, and will your sparks consciously into existence, then you'll be ahead of the eight ball.

GROWING PAINS

*G*rowing pains happen. They're an inevitability of change. A bi-product. A sunk cost. Those are the breaks. You get to the good by going through (not around) the bad. In the moment, they're necessary distractions that fill in the path between A & Z, with character building qualities you can keep. In the aftermath they serve as reminders of a tougher time, reflecting a journey that allows for appreciation and a sense of accomplishment. Prior to said accomplishment, growing pains serve as a deterrent. A thinner of hoards. An ideal that weeds out the masses and leaves you with the most determined and wanting individuals that embrace the growing pains affiliated with their goals as what they are … inevitably necessary truths.

PERPETUATE LIFE

*S*crape past the surface of living. Embrace life and all its fruits. Melt into all of the nuanced textures of existence. Re-Surface as a new and improved version of a built upon – you. Make every moment the moment that you're in. Remember to win, even when you lose. Choose forward and outward progress, based on focused and inward perspective. Have the belief in yourself to trust in the foresight and have the gumption to go for it, the determination to stick with it, the objectivity to not get lost in it, and the good fortune to reflect upon it all as you pass that blueprint on and perpetuate life.

YOUR CRAFT

*T*herapy for the mind. An out-pouring of the soul. An outlet for thought and emotion. A vehicle for creation. Manifesting the dreamt-of, and the unknown finding its way into existence with the clear focused determination of certainty. A certainty you weren't certain, was there. Once it exposes itself you guide it, it guides you. You nurture it, it fuels you. Pushing you from where you were, toward where it is you want to be and everything in between. It's a method of disposal. Removal of waste. Organizing of mental clutter. It's expression frozen in time, forever on the pages of the story of your life, followed by an unwritten future eagerly awaiting to be met.

ELEVATE YOURSELF

$\mathcal{M}$ake the next one better. The next ... everything. Whatever 'next' is or will be ... make it better. From the most menial task to an intricate more elaborate plan. Whatever you're doing now, whatever you're in front of ... do it better than the last time you did that particular thing. Examples? – Cutting your toenails, reading this book, writing a story, watching a movie, washing your hands, typing, driving, running, thinking, etc. You get the idea. Anything and everything is something that is/can be enhanced ... so do it better. Improve. This is how you elevate yourself. You know that feeling you get when moments after you've spoken to someone, (usually in passing but not necessarily), and you think of the "perfect thing you should've said" ... less of that. More new and improved versions of you, on every level. On a microbial, culture of flora, eco-systematic type of level. Making up a collectively enhanced version of you.

LUCK SEES WORK

*L*uck. A four letter one syllable word that can always be there and at the same time just not care. Like a sub-atomic particle in Quantum Theory both existing and not existing in separate places at the exact same time. Cloaked like a dagger with the possibility of piercing through and touching you. Wanting it, expecting it, chasing it, asking for it even. With an omniscient presence it undetectably weighs in on every endeavor … if it so chooses of course. How do you get in its good graces? How do you buddy-up to this force? With another four letter, one syllable word … work. It'll always be there. Atop the throne of possibility. Waiting for you to earn a sprinkle of its influence. You never know when or even if it'll ever chime in and lend a hand, but it favors the prepared and your hard work prepares you to pull yourself towards it. Make your own luck? – Not really. Make it so that luck notices you? – Absolutely.

WHAT IS INSPIRATION?

*I*nspiration is what I would imagine being in the barrel of a wave and riding the tube, feels like to a surfer. What a submission victory feels like to a grappler. The realization felt by a hunter who tracked and stalked his prey for days before their respective paths crossed. The feeling in the pit of the stomach of a drag racer who pulled off of the line so perfectly along with shifting in such pristine mechanical cadence that crossing that quarter-mile mark first is imminent. Inspiration is what I would imagine a game winning home-run feels like. A strike-out to solidify a win. A buzzer-beating shot. A unique, one of a kind frozen image of an instance in time, shuttered by a photographers camera. The final stroke of a brush on an artful canvas. An Oscar winning performance, mid-delivery. Ace-ing the exam and finishing that paper, to an academic. When you're on track to running the table in pool. The feeling you get that wafts over you when you listen to a worth-while song. Creating what will inspire with the same level of inspiration that fueled it.

BLIND LIMITATIONS

It flows through you right before the point of commitment. Between wanting it and demanding it. – Your passion does. Like an understanding or mutual commitment. Show me you want it and I'll give it to you. Earn your keep and you'll have more than you need. Passion and focus in abundance. An unlimited supply with an undiscriminating appetite akin to a W.M.D. – But with laser sharp precision. Taking out, effortlessly, anything you've set your mind to. That's what passion does. That's why desire exists. Turning a corner and embarking on a journey where even mistakes fund space and solace, because there's a place for them. Passion strikes me as a tunnel-vision confidence unaware of the possibility of its limitations.

PULL THE FUTURE
INTO THE PRESENT

*F*uck the light at the end of the tunnel. Rid yourself of the darkness you're in, now. Grab and pull the future into the present and begin to live tomorrow, today. Focus on what needs to be focused on and with the same intent, neglect what needs neglecting. Drop the excess baggage whether it be persons or things. Lose the weights that are holding you down. Nobody is necessarily necessary and neither is anything else. There are essentiality's to harboring life, and then there's everything else. Realize and come to terms with the fact that everyone else is in this game (for lack of a better word) too. Albeit for an array of different reasons. Reasons some of which will be like your own, and most others will not be. Borrow, accept and appreciate enhancements along the way and with the same level of intent. Dispel with great and severe prejudice any diminishment or possibility of deterioration in your way.

IT'S A CONSCIOUS DECISION

ake time to clear your mind and you will find the best way for you to unwind what wound you up so tight. Let the mess of the stress waft over you and pass. Go beyond the point of fury and frustration and find yourself in the center of reason ... for a reason. There is a most negative and a most positive way that any situation can unfold. That being said, why not put yourself into the best mind state to yield the benefits of the positive side of that spectrum? When thought of in hindsight it's almost a no-brainer, right? - To give yourself and those around you the benefits of the most positive outcome to any given situation. Take a step back from what you're going through and give yourself the objective conscious ability of positivity.

DON'T SAVE IT, SHARE IT.
DON'T HARBOR IT, RELEASE IT

Whenever inspiration hits you … it's probably not a conscious decision. It's more of an epiphany. Let it take its course. Let it ooze out of you in whatever form or medium it takes. Express it however it wants to be expressed. Release it. Let it out. Don't trap it, bottle it up and allow it to go stale. Don't harbor it and 'save it for later'… it won't be there later, at least not in the same way that it was. And the best part … it's infinite. Ever expanding. You couldn't waste it if you tried. Ride its wave and elevate yourself and possibly even others by doing so. How great of a 'plus' is that?! So whether it's a song, a quote, a book, a line in a movie, an instrumental solo, a laugh, an anything – that gives you a momentary glimpse into the self perpetuating purity that is inspiration … embrace it and run with it, because although the stream can't be – the moment can be wasted. Like a white light going through a prism and coming out of the other side as an array of different colors … allow it not only to enter you in that unexpected from, but also to come out of you in its desired form.

WALK YOUR PATH

*T*he combination of thoughts experiments and experiences that it takes to be you ... in this realm ... cannot be replicated. To allow fear and insecurity to blanket the innate selfishness that is *not* expressing yourself is a disservice to your evolution as a person, and to your influence on the evolution of others. How dare you take that cowardly route. Be you 24/7/365 (366 in a leap year) and don't you ever look back ... at least not in a questioning or resenting way. We shouldn't have a choice. Let the light that's inside you shine through. Let it light your path – the path that is walk-able by you and you alone. It's ok to find yourself and figure things out by going through different experiences in life, but it's not ok to find solace and comfort in one of those experiences and pigeonhole yourself into it solely for a sense of security. Shake things up until that sense of security is implicit and just part of the package deal realized by the second nature feeling that is living your dream. Follow your unique light.

SPARK THEIR VERSIONS OF

The realization of a passion in a moment of time. A snippet of existence, is what it's all about. Endorphins exuding out of your being. Positive and imperishable vibes breaking down obstacles, seeking out every ounce of doubt within every nook-and-cranny of yourself while simultaneously extinguishing any doubts expressed toward you. It's your moment and yours alone. Shareable with no other, although experience-able by many. They can't feel what you feel within your moment. It's a level of un-transferable elation that no amount of empathy could ever encapsulate. Realize your passions and experience them with those that you hold close to your heart ... they may not feel exactly what you feel, but it will spark their versions of.

IT'S NOT YOUR CALL TO SAY NO

When you "do", you will it into existence. There was no it before you. It is because of you, not in spite of you. Let it be, let it grow. It's in your power but not your call to say no. Who are you and why do you think it's up to you? Get out of the way and allow it to come thru. You'll never truly know who you're reaching and touching, but you are reaching and touching. Don't ever think it's up to you to deny your receivers of that possibility.

LET YOUR WORLD COME TO LIFE

*orning reps in the afternoon. Past due, a bit past noon. But fuck it, get it in. Lay it down. The foundation needs to be thick, an indestructible and humble ground. No sound as specific or style as prolifically you. There can't be. No … there literally *can't* be. So you owe it to us, I owe it to me, to go inside me. Come along for the ride with me while I ride within you. This is what we all need to do. The truest truth is within all of you and me too. Lets bring it out to the forefront already. What are we waiting for? Seriously stop and think … what are you waiting for? I bet you can't even pin point it, I know I couldn't. Just a foggy abstract version of a hazy 'one day' – and if you happen to have something(s) on the horizon keeping you at bay from seeing the sunrise … kill that noise immediately and let your world come to life.

INSPIRE GREATNESS

nspire greatness in yourself and others. Act with it in mind. With the mindset that obtaining the unobtainable goal *is* obtainable. Strive for excellence. Strive for perfection. Will you reach these? Probably not. Not in the absolute sense anyhow. So why strive for them? Why strive for anything? Because there is excellence, there is perfection … your version of these things. On this path that you're on, many will be touched. Some will draw inspiration from you and some will only tune into the negative aspects and pitfalls of your path. Either way, continue to be and strive to be the best version of yourself that you can create.

WE ARE ONE

here's no winning in the game of life. Conversely there is no losing. There's only (for lack of a better word) playing. There's no tangible need for keeping score, nor settling any. There's you and those around you. There's those that were and those that will be. All of which exist to the best or worst of their abilities, as they so choose. The shade they cast over their space in the world with their unique hue, is the mosaic nature that is the very essence of life. Our individual canvases co-exist, mix and intertwine. Build, fill and define yours with your version of perfection. Your best self. That immeasurable quality that is you. The infinite fluidity with which we grow and develop is far more precious than a win/lose game could ever hope to be. We've already won … we are one.

DON'T LET YOURSELF
WASTE AWAY

*D*on't wait based on the assumption that there will be more. You create more. What is it that's keeping you from doing what you want to be doing? Better still, what is it that's keeping you from realizing *what* it is that you want to be doing? [Insert your response here] ... and then do away with it. Make it powerless. Is it a person? Several people? A financial situation? A thought? A fear? Don't let yourself waste away. Whatever it is, flip it around. Need a certain level of financial status or stability? Then get a job (related or not) that will allow you to meet that need. Set that financial freedom goal and purchase your limitations. It's you. It always has been. You limit yourself when you could be limitless. Achieve your 'more' by locking yourself into this state:

THE FEARLESS EAGERNESS of an imaginative child,
    The ignorant confidence of a teenager and
    The humbling wisdom that comes with age.

THE WORTH IS IN
THE WILL TO DO IT

If I don't do it when I don't want to do it ... I'm not doing it when it counts. When I'm down and out, filled with doubt. Lacking motivation and drive. No will to strive for what's mine. When I rather hide from success because that's what feels best. Devoid of stress. Where's the value in that? Where's the worth? The worth is in the will to do what you want to do, when you don't want to do it. That's what makes the difference between talking about it and being about it. Don't give yourself any passes or freebees. Be harder on yourself than your worst critic would be, but forgive yourself unconditionally. The valleys allow for those peaks. That's how you get through the rough patches and set backs and build up the necessary momentum to cause a positive paradigm shift.

BE PRESENT. BE
INSPIRED. BE YOU.

Inspiring inspiration inspires me to be inspired. It fuels all. A universal remote, an all access pass. Inspiration truly does transcend all. It can be found in all things and it is generated and sparked from all things. Random as well as deliberate. I've found motivation in writing, in reading, in Podcasts, in songs, movies, television shows, stories and conversations. It can be found anywhere that you go looking … but you need to look. Sometimes in its vast abundance it blindsides you like the realization that you've slept thru your alarm. It can find you. You can be inspired at work and at play. Day or night. There's no discrimination in inspiration. It's inside you and all around you at the same time. It's love. It's God. It's family. It's presence. Be present. Be inspired. Be you.

KEEP IT FOREVER

ou'll make it when you don't ever make it. That's when you arrive. Keep grinding. Work, work and then work some more. Don't stop, except to look around and take it all in. You'll know it when you're there. Trust me. And when you get there, you'll be present enough to grind that much harder. Keep that momentum up by continuing what you're doing and not losing it ... then you get to keep it. Always. It's yours.

WRITING VS. HAVING WRITTEN

I read once that the distinction between a "real'" writer and poser, is the difference between wanting to write and wanting to have written. But which one makes you "real"? I want both minus the anxious anticipation of needing to write. Once I get myself to sit and do the work, and it's flowing ... there's not much else that's better. Once I complete a project, it's a feeling of accomplishment mixed with; I need to get better. And I will, right? Stick-to-itiveness has that effect on people and their abilities. So let me do both. Write and have written until what I have written becomes its best and when I write, I enjoy it no less. Maybe there, at that specific place, will the gap between writing and needing to, close.

OPEN YOUR MINDS EYE

✎

I kind of feel defeated, but it's motivating this time. No let down or disappointed theme in my thought process. More of a "get up, get out and get something[1]" type of feeling. Lets use that. Really use it to channel and aim toward specific points of needed improvement. This way, when and if the feeling fades and the motivation wanes, you can look back and see the benefits you reaped. The correlation between that feeling and what was improved. Don't lose that. Don't lose you. Take a deep breath, open up your minds eye, take aim and shoot.

---

1. The concept of a song by Outkast feat. Goodie Mob - Git Up Get Out

TIME'S PASSING BY WITH THE CONSISTENCY OF ALWAYS

*S*et a minuscule, minor goal. Make it achievable. Reach that, then repeat the process. I'll borrow from Tim Ferriss and start off with "two shitty pages per day". Gain some traction and expand on it. Times passing by with the consistency of always. The goals are good all fine and dandy, but they shouldn't be so far off from what is being worked on and put into practice. What good are 187 goals when you're sill working on goal #3. Stop tacking them on. It's time for action. Enough inaction. 'Get that work'. Penalize yourself by not allowing new add-ons to that goal-list until you bridge the gap between done and undone. Until you lower the spread. Otherwise you're just making plans to live without actually living out your plans. You deserve better and you know it. You can do better and you know that too.

YOUR ANSWERS ARE NOT WRITTEN. WRITE THEM.

rite your own answers. Questions are subjective by definition, and will always be more readily available. Doubt, fear of the unknown, and uncertainty all cloud your vision. They lead you to believe that answers exist and are already written, for each of your questions. You'll probably wind up searching for those answers and might even find some along the way. The questions you leave *un*answered you'll probably chalk up to not doing your due diligence … and you're partly right in thinking that way. Except it's not that you didn't find the answer(s) you were looking for. It's that you didn't realize that the answer for everything you're looking for is and will always be, within you. You just need to write it. The answer key to life is knowing that no question needs to remain unanswered. Search deep enough within yourself and the answers will reveal themselves.

FLOAT AIMLESSLY THROUGH LIFE, BUT IN A SPECIFIC DIRECTION OF YOUR CHOOSING

*S*tart where you will and end where you may. All else will fall into its respective place. As will you in a grander scheme of things. Can you take aim at the place(s) you want to land? And if you could … would you pull the trigger? Try and balance this out in your mind: float aimlessly through life, but in a specific direction of your choosing. Care enough up until the point of dependency. Beyond that point, there's no return. Stop wasting the time in between.

CHANGE YOUR STARS

❧

hy do we get caught up in the chaotic details of the "fluff"? Is it necessary? Do we have to for some balance and the ability to enjoy the alternatives? Fuck, what a waste of time. When it's all said and done and we look back on the legacy of our individual lives … what do you want to see? Politics? Corporate ladder climbing? Your place(s) within the cog of the machine? Yea, me either. All that fluff needs to become a means to an end. Not the actual end. Lets not let it end like this. "Change your stars[1]".

---

1. This is a quote about changing your life for the better, from the movie; A Knights Tale

FEARLESSLY GRASP THE FUTURE

*C*an you feel it? Can you see it coming? The zeitgeist of our time is awe. Inspiring minds to believe again. To think further than ever before. To understand deeper than we've ever dared. Are you ready to achieve all you've ever wanted? Lets do it! Work towards it. Earn it. "The beginning is near[1]" and we're approaching it with a fearless ferocity. The momentum is with us. It's on our side. Like a tidal wave waiting to splash and crescendo into any rocks that stand in our way. Pursue greatness. Strive for excellence. And appreciate the grace by which we're grasping the future.

---

1. This is a quote from Art by the Imaginary Foundation

BE HUMBLE

*ocusing on what others have that you don't have, is an exercise in futility. Instead, practice humility. Be happy for those that have more, feel bad for those that have less and find solace in what you do have. That's not to say you can't or shouldn't want more for yourself and others around you, you absolutely can and should. But elevate yourself to the point of your desires, through hard work, focus discipline and dedication. Have the gumption to go through the rough patches, so that you deserve to reap the fruits of your labor. Don't give up on your goals.

MAINTAIN HUMILITY
THROUGHOUT YOUR JOURNEY

Think about where you want to be in 5, 10, 20 years. Now stop and look at where you're at now. You won't make it to where you want to be without focused dedication and hard work during the period in between. Step out of the way of resistance,[1] tuck away doubt, implement ambition with a sprinkle of the confidence of knowing you belong where you want to be … they just don't know it yet. But boy will they. Maintain humility throughout your journey if you want to be worthy of the fruits of your labor. That grounding ingredient is the fertilizer that will allow the growth of your future.

---

1. The concept of Resistance as a force is from my favorite book: The War of Art by Steven Pressfield.

ELEVATE YOUR THOUGHTS

*W*here are you headed? What are your plans? Your thoughts about the future? Your dreams? Any concerns? What would you do differently if you had unlimited re-do's? And if you didn't correct some of your past errors, will you be where you're at now? Thinking the same thought? I'd like to think so. Just a more elevated version of the core, true you. Making even sharper, crisper decisions that are exponentially ascending. Elevate your thoughts to no bounds. Beyond your past mistakes. Keep the history of who you are and couple that with the you that you always wanted to be.

START OFF THE DAY WITH
SOMETHING THAT YOU LOVE

❧

*S*et serious time aside for what you want to be doing in life. When you wake up every morning, make it the first thing that you do. Why not start off the day with something that you love? Have to wake up and go to work? So wake up earlier to do what you love and start the day off right. If not, stop kidding yourself. You have a full time job and a part time hobby ... lets work on flipping that equation. Set specific time apart for your part time hobby and make it a part time job. We have to put in that level of work to make it to the next stage. Then with enough work and dedication, that hobby that we love will transition from a part-time job to a full time job, replacing the full time job we had because of necessity. Then voilà ... we wind up with a full time hobby. Sounds perfect to me. Let's give it a whirl.

IT WILL NOT BE FOR NAUGHT

*S*ometimes it's shit. Most of the time actually. It can't always be a gem. Unless its perceived, received and interpreted in just the right way that it's needed. But what are the chances of that? In the mean time, just put your head down. Let it flow. Let it overflow. Your cup will surely runneth over. Let it spill, soak and seep into the consciousness of the collective psyche. Then one day, stop. Turn around and take a look at the collage of life experiences that you've left behind. It'll mean something to someone … even if that someone is you.

DON'T WORRY

hen you begin to worry, stop. Take a deep breathe. Think about what your worrying is accomplishing. After you determine the inevitable answer: Nothing, move on to focusing your time, energy and emotional state towards fixing whatever it was/is that made you so upset. Start with the root cause; How did this happen? What caused the occurrence to take place ... then, take the proper steps to eliminate that catalyst. A lot of what we worry about and concern ourselves with is fixable with the correct approach. The things that aren't in our control, that we tend to worry about ... the 'bigger' things, wont shift in either direction due to our worrying ... so focus on positioning yourself to be in a better state of mind and place to handle the repercussions as they occur. Easier said than done, but doable.

IT ALL PASSES

Its been real. Its been epic. But all good things, and bad as well, must come to an end. Don't worry though … not even for a millisecond, for the end of each era just gives you a set of keys to unlock the doors of multiple future possibilities. Take what you've learned here, both the good and the bad, tuck it into your arsenal and let your heart point you in the next direction, while your experiences guide you through. Don't ever lose hope. Make us both that promise. Even the darkest days brighten up. It all passes. Maybe not absolutely, but sufficiently. Hurt and pain will be hurt and pain. But hope and prosperity will be hope and prosperity. Love will be Love. We're all on a journey that seems to be searching for truth and meaning and pride. This right here is just a moment within a chapter in that journey. We all have our experiences to go through and they may not always be experiences we wanted or asked for. – But they're necessary. For our development and for the development of those around us. Please don't lose that hope, it's essential to it all. Keep growing in your way, so that our paths can once again intertwine.

THANK YOU WRITING

You'll always lend a listening ear. You know what I'm going to say before I even know that I want to say it. You phrase things in a way that may not even make sense to you, but that are so eloquently me. You're there for me even when I'm not there for you. Selfless. You always great me with passion treat me with compassion and say goodbye with a sincere and evident longing. I'm not deserving of you even when I'm willing to give all there is to give of me … it's not enough. I don't feel like it's worthy. But to you … it's always plenty. They say you get what you give but that's clearly not a truth. You've given me infinitely more than an eternity would ever allow me to repay. You bring me out of myself and stand beside me as you show me the way. No ulterior motives or plans to lead me astray. Zero expectations, when you could expect the cosmos in return. Your unparalleled benevolence is humbling. I love you, writing … and strive to be as righteous, virtuous and noble as you.

RATE & REVIEW

Did you enjoy this read?
Please don't forget to rate & review it at your favorite online retailer!

ABOUT THE AUTHOR

Tony Ortiz is a first-generation Dominican American born in Brooklyn and raised in Queens, New York. He is the host of the *Spun Today* Podcast, which is anchored in writing but unlimited in scope. He is a graduate of Baruch College in NYC and lives in Queens, New York with his wife and two sons.

Let's stay in touch!
Twitter/X: @SpunToday
Instagram: @SpunToday
YouTube: @SpunToday
Facebook: www.Facebook.com/SpunToday

Sign up to my free weekly newsletter for a little boost to your day every Monday at noon. You can unsubscribe at any time, but you won't want to. (I won't bombard you with spam, promise!)

www.SpunToday.com/subscribe

THE SPUN TODAY PODCAST

Listen to my Podcast

Looking for a podcast that will take you on a thrilling ride of creativity and exploration? Look no further than the Spun Today Podcast which is anchored in Writing but unlimited in scope. Hosted by Tony Ortiz, this show is a celebration of the art of writing, and so much more. With an endless range of interests and topics, Tony invites you to join him on a journey through the world of movies, books, TV shows, stand-up comedy, politics, current events, interviews and beyond. Whether you're a fan of the written word or just looking for an exciting new podcast to add to your playlist, the Spun Today Podcast is the perfect choice. So why wait? Give it a whirl today and experience it for yourself!

Listen on Apple Podcasts, Spotify, YouTube, my website, or your favorite Pod-Catcher.

ACKNOWLEDGMENTS

To my father, Segundo Antonio Ortiz. You're the cornerstone of it all, Pop. You showed me that actions speak louder than words ever could. Thank you for teaching me the merits of integrity, discipline, responsibility, and hard work. These are invaluable character traits that I promise to pass on to the next generation. Making you proud means everything to me.

To my mother, Diomeda "Meme" Ortiz. Thank you for showing me humility and compassion. You've selflessly given all there is to give of you and truly made us a family. Your belief in me has always given me a reason to believe in myself.

To my big bro, David Ortiz. You've been hard on me when I didn't even know I needed you to be. For a long time, I felt like you were my biggest critic, until I realized you were by far my number one supporter. Thank you for always having my back and know that without hesitation I'll always have yours.

To my wife and babzy, Zoila Ortiz. If it wasn't for you, I probably wouldn't have ever taken this writing thing seriously. You made it all come together for me by giving me the nudge I needed to get on this journey, and you've been there every step of the way. Thank you for your unwavering kindness, unconditional love, and for showing me the importance of laughter. I had forgotten that some time ago. You're my favorite person to be around and you constantly make me want to be a better me.

To my high school freshman English teacher, Ms. Lisa Gittlitz. You knew I should be writing before I ever did. I wish I would have listened more. Thank you for caring enough to always encourage this hard-headed teen and for making me write all those Lit-Logs.

To Maciel Chatterjee. If it weren't for you and a random conversation we had on an idle (I want to say Saturday) afternoon, I probably wouldn't have found the catharsis that comes with free-writing. Thank you for teaching me what it was and for always being a friend. I still have that first piece you got me to write.

The Joe Rogan Experience Podcast was the motivating straw that broke the procrastinating camel's back for me. It has been a hub of fascinating conversations, inspiration, fun times, and life lessons. Not only did it make me realize that it was okay to pursue my dreams, but it gave me the necessary kick in the ass to realize that they were all possible too. It's truly a gift that each of you should unwrap. Joe, Brian, Jaime, and every guest who has and continues to share their experiences on the show…thank you. I am eternally grateful.

I heard Elliott Hulse speak of the three types of people in our lives (you can find the video on YouTube). I reflected on the relationships in my life and found there to be a lot of truth to this. The concept really resonated with me. The gist of it is that the people in your life generally fall under one of these three categories:

Crystal balls: These are people through which you can see your future. Through them you ask yourself if you want to experience and characterize what this person represents, in your own future. Good, bad, or neutral.

Mirrors: These are people who give you back what you give them. You may see in them similar traits or goals and ambitions, which cause you to enjoy each other's company. Or you see people you're repelled by, and these can be people who themselves are reflecting back to you, traits in yourself that you need to address and rectify.

Angels: These are people who positively impact your life knowingly or not, and whether you're ready to receive their blessing(s) or not.

Each of you have touched my life in a significant way somewhere along the line, and fall under some combination of the above:

Steven Almonte (the definition of a hustler), Frank "Steve" Padilla (thank you for being family), Jonathan Jacob (the only person I can reconnect with every couple years and have it feel as if we spoke the day before, without skipping a beat), Arnaldo Coutinho (a true mentor), Jose Luis Oliveira (who taught me: "don't leave for tomorrow what you can get done today"), Yudy Azurdia (la mejor decoradora), Jacey Rosa (who has the best laugh), Raul Azurdia (the #1 Roomy), Omar "Jerry Rivera" Fuentes, Janet Velez (who deserves a trophy for holding down my brother), Jorge Nobre (thanks for going out of your way to drive me back from Mineola to Queens when we worked at the bar together), Benny Collado (blairwitz), Elaine Almonte (who I can always count on for an objective writing critique), Esrin Garcia (for teaching me how to really drive a stick-shift), Pablo Mosquera (for teaching me to grab life by the handlebars - RIP), Peter Cepeda, Virginia Florentino, Raul Lizardo, Rafael Polanco, David "Energizer" Carvalho, Roberto Prudencio (*jó Algarve!*), Arturo Flores (RIP), Dr. Arthur Lewin (my ambassador of Black & Latino studies), Jessica Florentino, Don Eladio (RIP), Doña Ana, Marisol & Antonio Almeida, Juana "Titi Mery" Susana, Maria "Titi Maro" Susana, Rafael "Mickey" Susana (RIP), Pedro "Julio" Susana, Ligia Reynoso, Francisco Reynoso (*da tuyo*), Antonia Susana, Isabel Susana, Reina "Tía Tata" Ortiz, Ygnacio Susana, Daniel Susana, Nicol Susana, Claribel & Julie Lizardo, Mary Reyes, Leonel Lucas, Abismael Gonzalez, Vicente Gonzalez *y todos mis Tíos, Tías, primos y familia.*

And last but certainly not least the future generation of the Ortiz Clan:

To my niece and goddaughter, Emma Ortiz. You have a heart of gold, and it shows. Don't let anyone or anything ever make you feel as if that's a bad thing. It's your greatest strength, and the future generation of our family is lucky to have you leading it.

To my niece, Olivia Ortiz. You're full of life and have a smile that brightens up any room. Keep smiling even when you're sad and know how infectious it is. You make others happier just by being around.

To both of my boys, which are pieces of my heart on the outside of my body:

To my big boy, Aiden Ortiz. You're an absolute blessing. My hope for you is that this book helps you realize there are alternative pathways you can take toward your version of happiness, and if you're willing to work 2, 3, 4 times as hard, you won't have to compromise responsibility to achieve it, either. Like your grandpa always said, *"Todo se puede hacer dentro de las reglas."* Thank you for looking at me with the kindest eyes in the world. I love you.

To my baby boy, Grayson Ortiz. You know what you want and you're going to get it. Just make sure you channel that energy wisely and never lose the essence of you in the process of chasing down your dreams. Continue to be as thoughtful as you are. That's a strength of yours. Choose that charming smile of yours and go in the direction of your happiness. Thank you for letting me in. I love you.

SUBSTITUTE THE MYSTICISM
WITH HARD WORK, AND START
TAKING STEPS IN THE GENERAL
DIRECTION OF YOUR DREAMS.

Answers for Lesson 5

Activity 1

1. b
2. a
3. c
4. a
5. b
6. c

Activity 3

1. give up
2. get back
3. point out
4. give up
5. get back

Activity 4

1. back
2. up
3. back
4. out
5. up
6. out

BE PRESENT WITHIN
YOUR CREATION

❧

*A*t least give yourself a chance to fail enough to succeed. It'll suck at times, sure ... but it doesn't always have to. Find appreciation in the process. After all, the bad times are just part of the charm. Whether your creation is to your liking or not. Good or bad by anyones measure. What you intended it to be or not ... it's more about *having created*. You know that feeling you get of something being there that wasn't before? - And it existing because of you? That's what it's all for. Keep battling through the rough patches. Continue to create existence. Exist and be present within your creation.